My Personal DICTIONARY

4th Edition

NEW SOUTH WALES

This book belongs to:

_____

OXFORD
UNIVERSITY PRESS
AUSTRALIA & NEW ZEALAND

Top 50 words in alphabetical order

a	home	she
and	house	so
are	I	that
at	in	the
because	is	then
but	it	there
can	like	they
dad	love	time
day	me	to
for	mum	was
fun	my	we
go	of	weekend
got	on	went
had	one	when
have	play	with
he	said	you
her	saw	

All about me

My name is _____

I live at _____

_____

My school is _____

My birthday is on _____

My favourite colour is _____

My favourite food is _____

My favourite game is _____

My special toy is _____

My best friend is _____

The alphabet

Aa	Jj	Ss
Bb	Kk	Tt
Cc	Ll	Uu
Dd	Mm	Vv
Ee	Nn	Ww
Ff	Oo	Xx
Gg	Pp	Yy
Hh	Qq	Zz
Ii	Rr	

Aa	Jj	Ss
Bb	Kk	Tt
Cc	Ll	Uu
Dd	Mm	Vv
Ee	Nn	Ww
Ff	Oo	Xx
Gg	Pp	Yy
Hh	Qq	Zz
Ii	Rr	

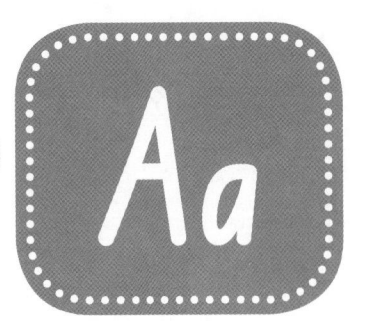

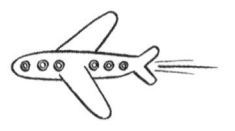

Aa

aeroplane   ape   apple

a	any
about	are
after	around
again	as
ago	asked
all	at
also	ate
always	aunty
am	away
amazing	awesome
an	
and	
animal	
animals	
another	

Aa
Bb
Cc
Dd
Ee
Ff
Gg
Hh
Ii
Jj
Kk
Ll
Mm
Nn
Oo
Pp
Qq
Rr
Ss
Tt
Uu
Vv
Ww
Xx
Yy
Zz

Bb

banana  bear  bus

baby	big	bubbles
back	bike	built
bad	bird	bunny
bag	birds	bus
ball	birthday	but
bat	bit	buy
be	black	by
beach	blue	
bear	book	
beautiful	books	
because	bought	
bed	box	
been	boy	
before	breakfast	
best	brother	

Aa
Bb
Cc
Dd
Ee
Ff
Gg
Hh
Ii
Jj
Kk
Ll
Mm
Nn
Oo
Pp
Qq
Rr
Ss
Tt
Uu
Vv
Ww
Xx
Yy
Zz

Cc

candle celery chimpanzee

cage	city	cute
cake	class	
called	clothes	
came	clown	
can	cold	
can't	colour	
car	come	
cars	coming	
castle	cool	
cat	could	
cats	couldn't	
cheese	cousin	
chicken	cousins	
chips	cow	
chocolate	crazy	

Dd

dice  *dolphin*  *drum*

dad	doll
dad's	don't
dancing	door
dark	down
day	dragon
days	
dear	
did	
didn't	
died	
different	
dinner	
do	
dog	
dogs	

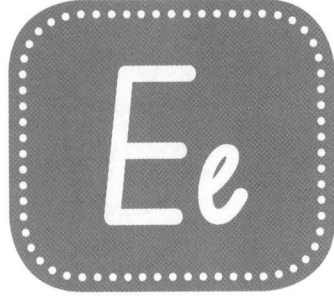

Ee

eagle    Earth 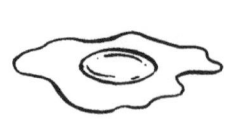   egg

| each |
| eat |
| egg |
| eggs |
| end |
| even |
| ever |
| every |
| everyone |
| everything |
| evil |
| excited |
| eyes |

Ff

football　　flag　　forest

face	flying	fruit
fairy	food	fun
family	football	funny
farm	footy	
fast	for	
favourite	forest	
fell	found	
felt	four	
finally	fox	
find	Friday	
finished	friend	
fire	friend's	
first	friends	
fish	frog	
fly	from	

Gg

giraffe glue grapes

game	grandma
games	grass
garden	great
gave	green
get	grown
getting	guinea pig
ghost	
giant	
girl	
give	
go	
goes	
going	
good	
got	

Hh

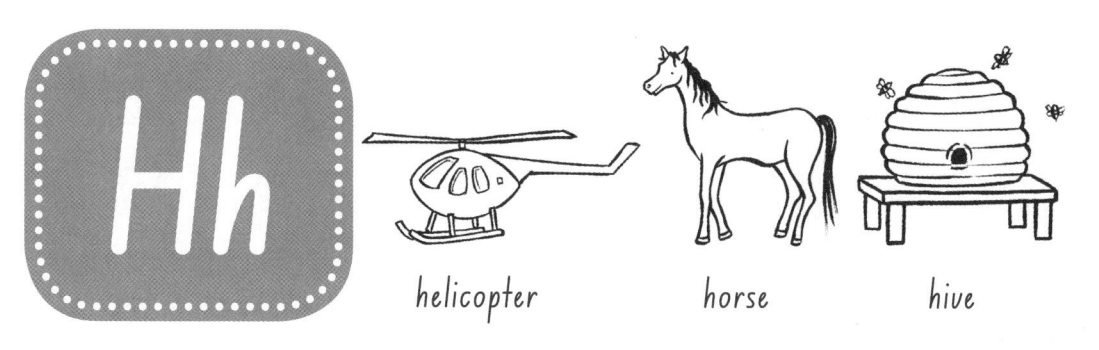

helicopter   horse   hive

had	here	
hair	hi	
half	hide	
hand	him	
happily	his	
happy	hit	
has	holiday	
have	holidays	
having	home	
he	hope	
head	hot	
hear	house	
heard	how	
help	hungry	
her		

Ii

ice   igloo   ice cream

I		
ice		
ice cream		
if		
I'll		
I'm		
in		
inside		
into		
is		
it		
it's		
its		

Jj

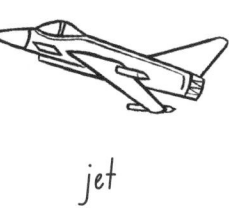

jet   jelly beans   juggler

jump
jumped
jungle
just

Kk

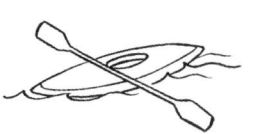

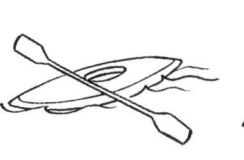

kayak   king   koala

kangaroo
kick
kids
kind
king
know

Ll

letter 　　lighthouse 　　lion

land	long	
last	look	
later	looked	
left	looking	
let	lost	
let's	lot	
life	lots	
light	love	
like	loved	
liked	lunch	
likes		
little		
live		
lived		
lollies		

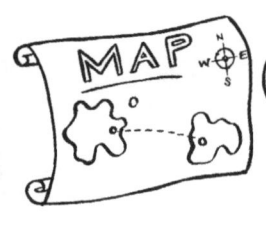

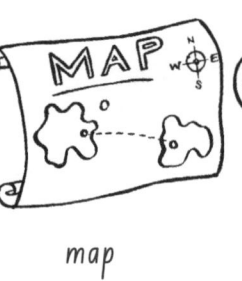

Mm

map   monkey   mouse

made	most	
magic	movie	
make	movies	
man	Mr	
many	much	
me	mum	
met	mummy	
might	music	
Miss	my	
Monday		
money		
monkey		
monster		
more		
morning		

Nn

nail newspaper noodles

name		
named		
names		
need		
never		
new		
next		
nice		
night		
no		
not		
now		
number		

Oo

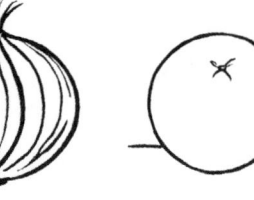

onion orange owl

of	over	
off		
oh		
OK		
old		
on		
once		
one		
only		
opened		
or		
other		
our		
out		
outside		

Pp

photo · pig · pizza

paper	playing
park	police
party	pool
people	pretty
person	princess
pet	puppy
pets	put
pig	
pigs	
pink	
pizza	
place	
play	
played	
playground	

Qq

queen   question mark   quilt

queen

Rr

robot   rocket   rollerblade

rabbit	room	
rabbits	run	
rain	running	
rainbow		
ran		
rats		
read		
reading		
really		
red		
ride		
riding		
right		
road		
robot		

Ss

scissors seal soccer ball

sad	she	so
said	sheep	soccer
same	shop	some
sat	shopping	someone
Saturday	shops	something
saw	show	sometimes
say	sick	soon
scared	side	spider
scary	sister	started
school	sleep	stay
sea	sleepover	stayed
second	slide	still
see	small	stop
set	snake	story
shark	snow	stuff

Ss

snake sphere sheep

suddenly
sun
Sunday
super
swimming

Tt

think   toybox   train

take	there	told
tea	they	too
teacher	thing	took
team	things	top
teeth	think	town
tell	this	toy
ten	thought	toys
than	three	train
thank	through	tree
that	tiger	trees
that's	time	tried
the	times	turned
their	to	TV
them	today	two
then	together	

Tt

tree tiger tablet

Uu

umbrella umpire unicorn

under
unicorn
until
up
upon
us
use

Vv

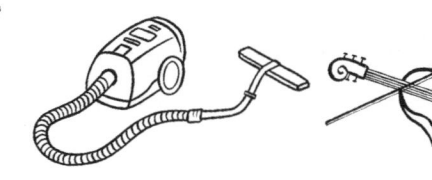

vase — vacuum cleaner — violin

very

Ww

waves watermelon witch

wait	weekend	wish
walk	well	witch
walked	went	with
walking	were	woke
want	what	wolf
wanted	when	won
was	where	wood
wasn't	which	work
watch	while	world
watched	white	would
watching	who	writing
water	whole	
way	why	
we	will	
week	win	

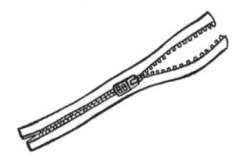

Xx	Yy	Zz
X-ray	yacht	zip
	year	zoo
	years	
	yellow	
	yes	
	yesterday	
	you	
	your	
	yummy	

Short 'a' sound rhyming words

—at	—an	—ap
bat	can	cap
hat	fan	clap
mat	man	map
sat	ran	tap

Short 'e' sound rhyming words

—ed	—en	—et
bed	hen	jet
fed	men	let
red	pen	net
shed	ten	pet

Short 'i' sound rhyming words

_ill	_ip	_it
bill	lip	exit
mill	sip	hit
pill	skip	quit
spill	tip	sit

Short 'o' sound rhyming words

—og	—op	—ot
bog	cop	cot
dog	crop	dot
jog	mop	hot
log	top	pot

Short 'u' sound rhyming words

_ub	_ug	_un
cub	bug	bun
grub	jug	fun
rub	mug	run
tub	rug	sun

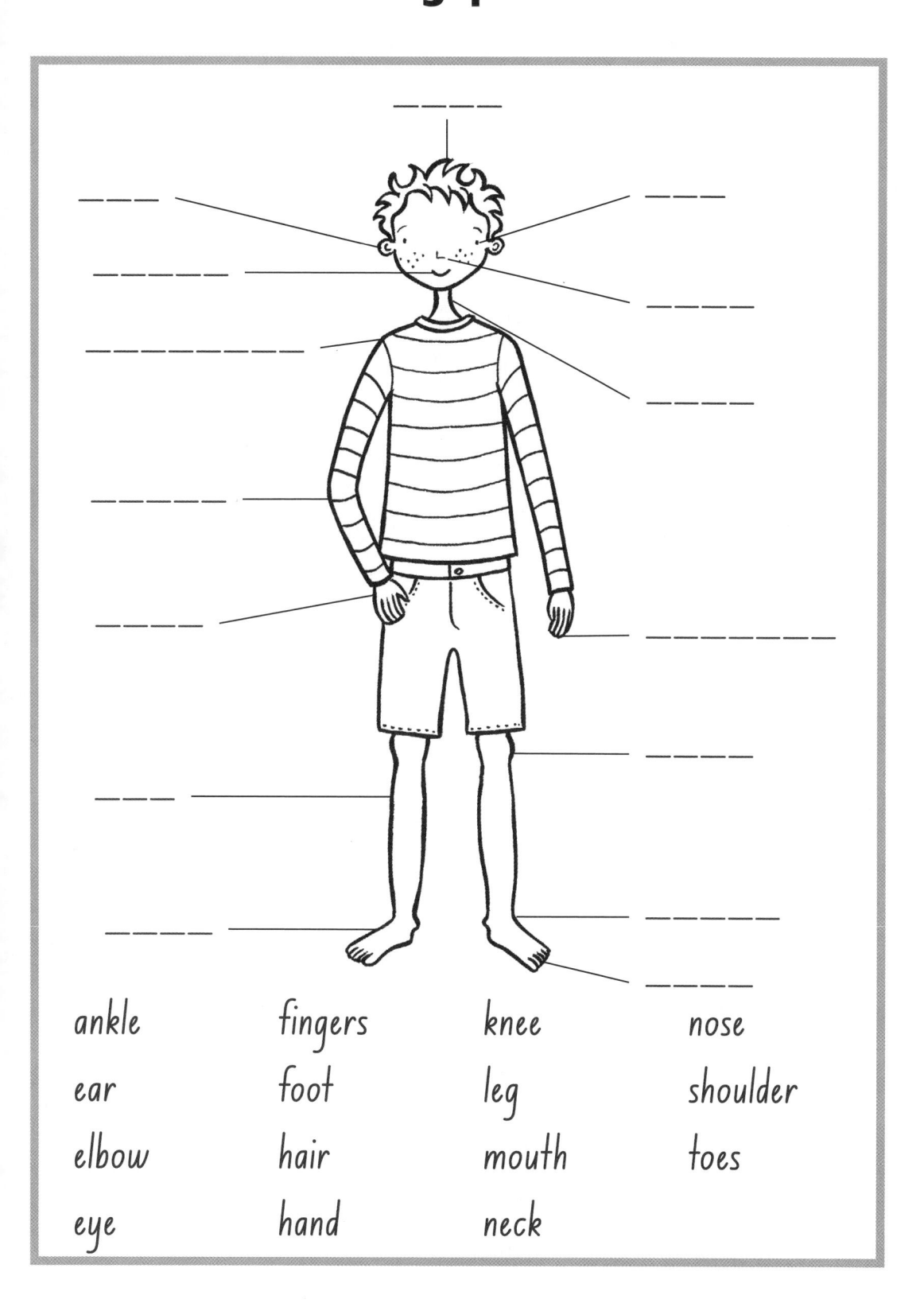

Body parts

ankle	fingers	knee	nose
ear	foot	leg	shoulder
elbow	hair	mouth	toes
eye	hand	neck	

Animals around the world

cow
calf

horse
foal

hen
chick

pig
piglet

sheep
lamb

giraffe

rhinoceros

panda

hippopotamus

lion

gorilla

African elephant

Indian elephant

38

bear

alligator

tiger

koala

wombat

little penguin

kangaroo

emperor penguin

dog
puppy

cat
kitten

goose
gosling

duck
duckling

goat
kid

39

Space

Sun
Mercury
satellite
Venus
Moon
Earth
shuttle
astronaut
space station
Mars
Jupiter
orbit
Saturn
Uranus
meteor
Neptune
star

People in our community

police officer

doctor   nurse

firefighter

farmer

paramedics

vet

dentist

teacher

builder

Australia

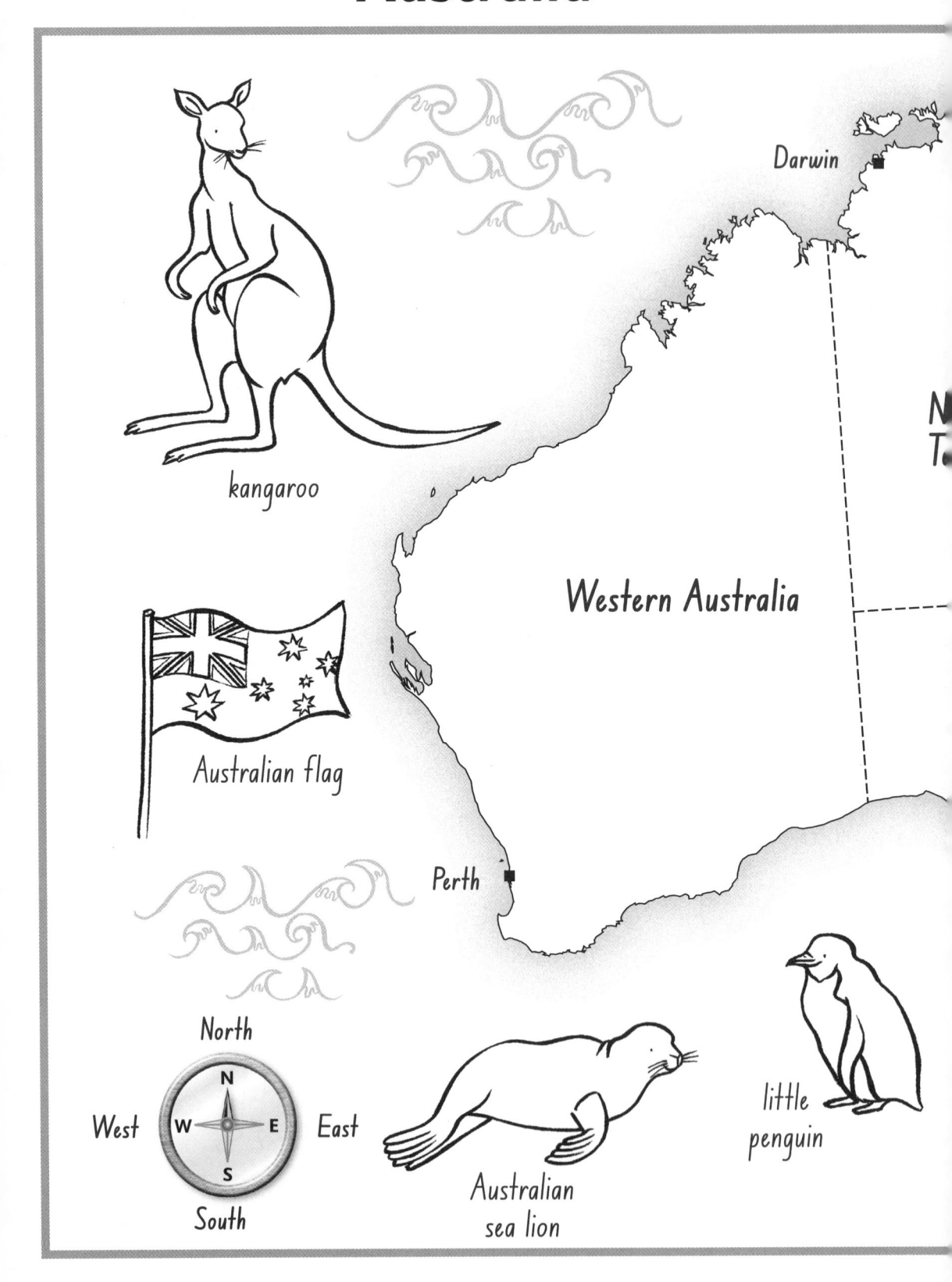

kangaroo

Australian flag

Darwin

Western Australia

Perth

North
West East
South

Australian sea lion

little penguin

42

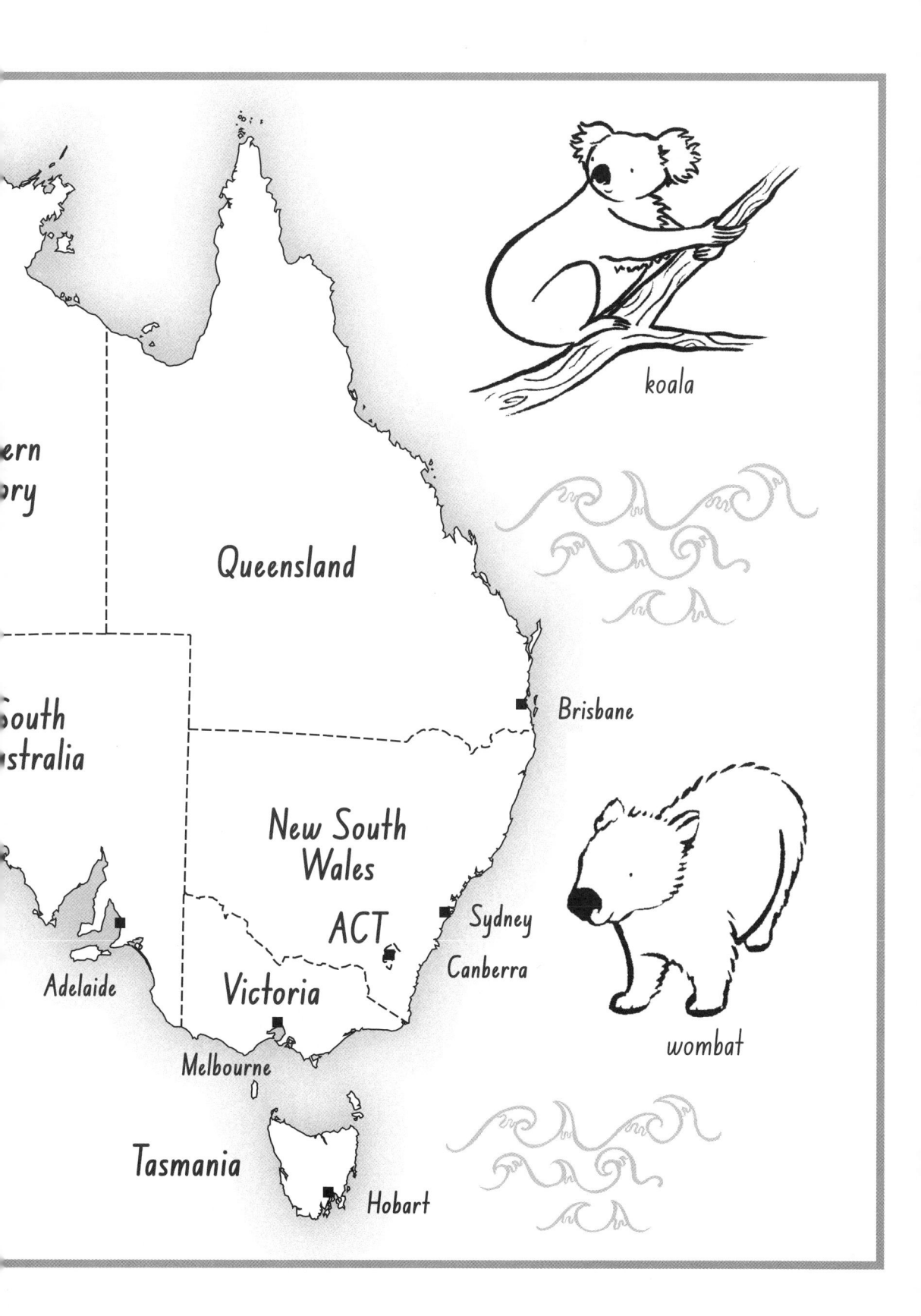

koala

Queensland

South
Australia

Brisbane

New South
Wales

ACT

Sydney
Canberra

wombat

Adelaide

Victoria

Melbourne

Tasmania

Hobart

43

Number words

1		one
2		two
3		three
4		four
5		five
6		six
7		seven
8		eight
9		nine
10		ten

11 eleven	17 seventeen	50 fifty
12 twelve	18 eighteen	60 sixty
13 thirteen	19 nineteen	70 seventy
14 fourteen	20 twenty	80 eighty
15 fifteen	30 thirty	90 ninety
16 sixteen	40 forty	100 one hundred

Shape words

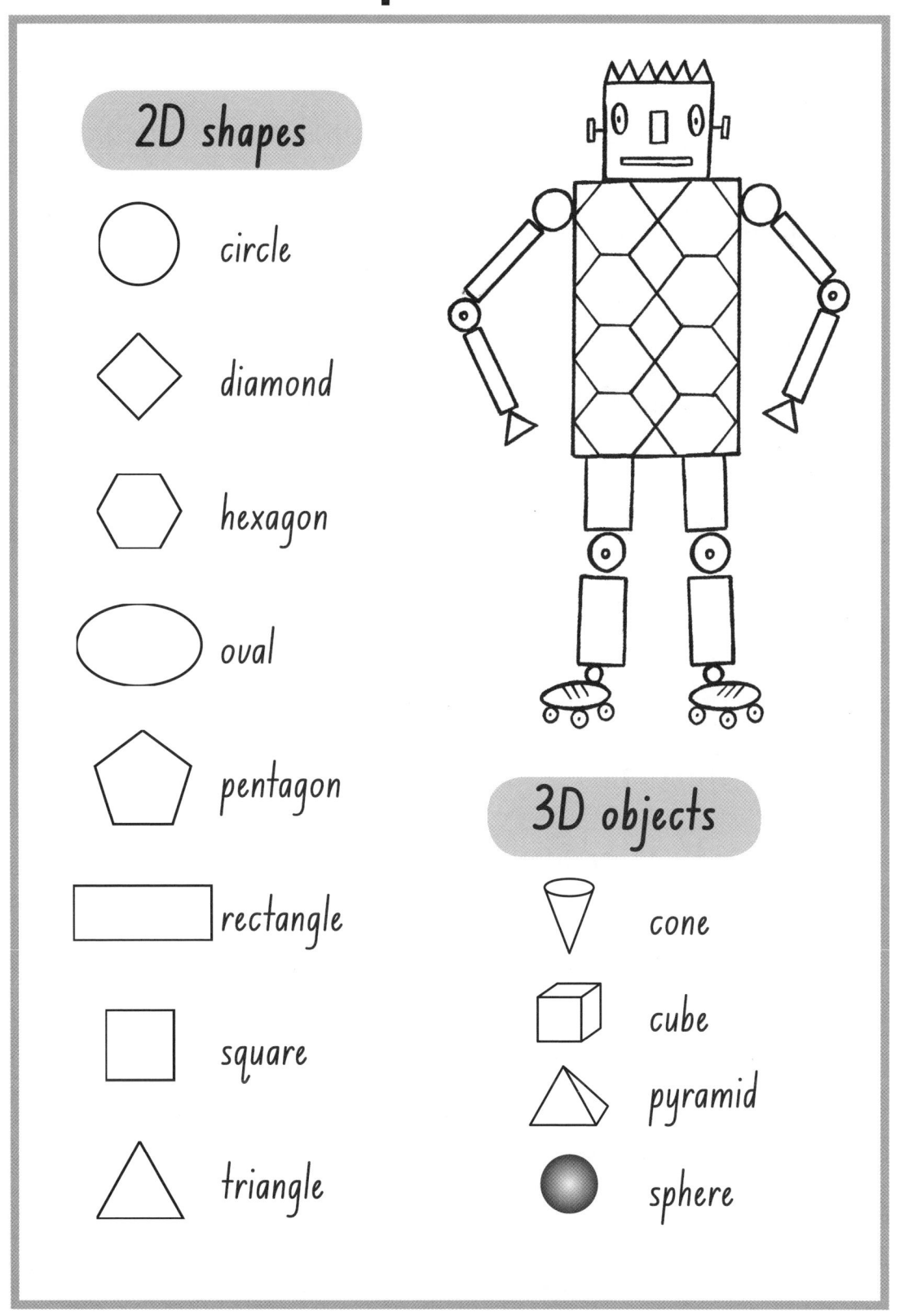

2D shapes

- ○ circle
- ◇ diamond
- ⬡ hexagon
- ⬭ oval
- ⬠ pentagon
- ▭ rectangle
- □ square
- △ triangle

3D objects

- cone
- cube
- pyramid
- sphere

Time words

day   week   month   year
hour   minute second

Days of the week

calendar

Monday
Tuesday
Wednesday
Thursday
Friday
WEEKEND
Saturday | Sunday

Seasons and months of the year

Summer
December
January
February

Autumn
March
April
May

Spring
September
October
November

Winter
June
July
August

Technology words

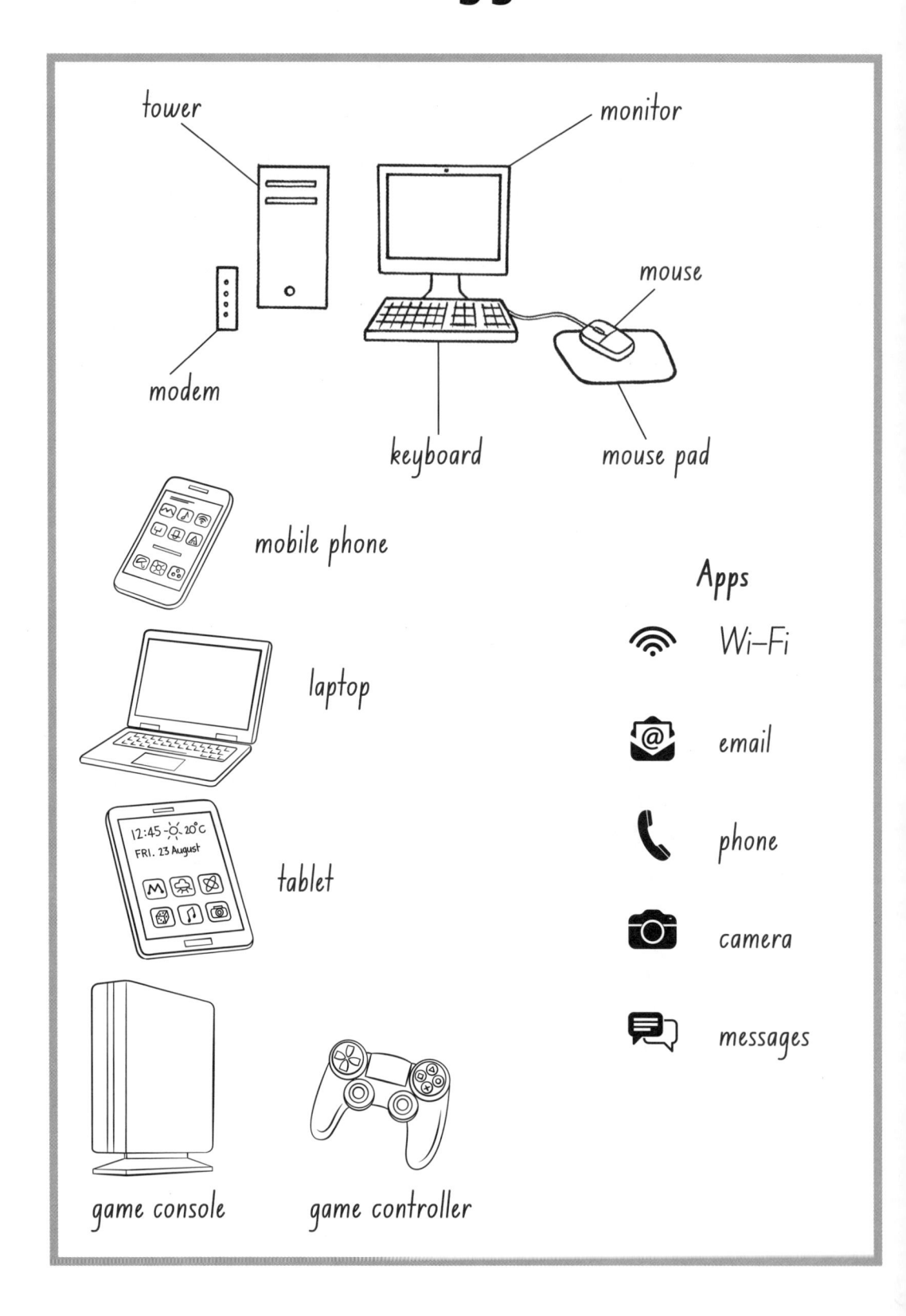

- tower
- monitor
- mouse
- modem
- keyboard
- mouse pad
- mobile phone
- laptop
- tablet
- game console
- game controller

Apps

- Wi-Fi
- email
- phone
- camera
- messages